LET'S EXPLORE THE STATES

Southern New England

Connecticut
Massachusetts
Rhode Island

Tish Davidson

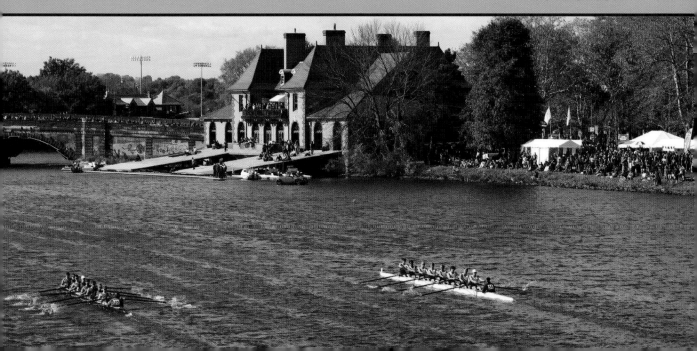

Mason Crest
450 Parkway Drive, Suite D
Broomall, PA 19008
www.masoncrest.com

©2016 by Mason Crest, an imprint of National Highlights, Inc.

Printed and bound in the United States of America.

CPSIA Compliance Information: Batch #LES2015.
For further information, contact Mason Crest at 1-866-MCP-Book.

First printing
1 3 5 7 9 8 6 4 2

Library of Congress Cataloging-in-Publication Data

    Davidson, Tish.
    Southern New England : Connecticut, Massachusetts, Rhode Island / Tish Davidson.
       pages cm. — (Let's explore the states)
    Includes bibliographical references and index.
    ISBN 978-1-4222-3333-7 (hc)
    ISBN 978-1-4222-8618-0 (ebook)
    1. Northeastern States—Juvenile literature. 2. Connecticut—Juvenile literature.
    3. Massachusetts—Juvenile literature. 4. Rhode Island Juvenile literature. I. Title.
    F106.D258 2015
    974—dc23
                         2014050199

Let's Explore the States series ISBN: 978-1-4222-3319-1

Publisher's Note: Websites listed in this book were active at the time of publication. The publisher is not responsible for websites that have changed their address or discontinued operation since the date of publication. The publisher reviews and updates the websites each time the book is reprinted.

About the Author: Tish Davidson has written many articles for newspapers and magazines. Her books for middle school readers include *African American Scientists and Inventors*, *Theocracy*, and *Facing Competition*. Davidson graduated from the College of William and Mary and earned a master's degree from Dartmouth College. She lives in Fremont, California.

Picture Credits: Architect of the Capitol: 31; ARENA Creative: 10; Office of the Governor of Massachusetts: 37 (bottom); John F. Kennedy Presidential Library and Museum, Boston: 38; Library of Congress: 13 (top), 14, 15, 16 (top right), 35, 40 (top), 54; The Nathanael Greene Homestead: 53; National Archives: 13 (bottom), 16 (top left); "The Whites of Their Eyes," Ken Riley / National Guard Heritage Series: 33; National Park Service: 34; Rhode Island Department of Public Works: 56; used under license from Shutterstock, Inc.: 6, 20, 24, 25, 37 (top), 39, 43, 46, 49, 57, 58; Richard Cavalleri/Shutterstock.com: 9, 18 (top), 23, 27 (bottom); Helga Esteb/Shutterstock.com: 60 (bottom); Featureflash/Shutterstock.com: 40 (bottom); Sasha Fenix/Shutterstock.com: 29; Jeffrey M. Frank/Shutterstock.com: 28, 50; Donald Gargano/Shutterstock.com: 12; Stephen B. Goodwin/Shutterstock.com: 51 (bottom); Aubrey Gough/Shutterstock.com: 21; Jaguar PS/Shutterstock.com: 16 (bottom); Ritu Manoj Jethani/Shutterstock.com: 22, 55; John Kropewnicki/Shutterstock.com: 1; Stuart Monk/Shutterstock.com: 5 (top); Sean Pavone/Shutterstock.com: 19; Christopher Penler/Shutterstock.com: 41; Henryk Sadura/Shutterstock.com: 42 (bottom); Jorge Salcedo/Shutterstock.com: 42 (top); Daniel M. Silva/Shutterstock.com: 51 (top); Marcio Jose Bastos Silva/Shutterstock.com: 5 (bottom), 30; Laura Stone/Shutterstock.com: 18 (bottom); Alex Svirid/Shutterstock.com: 44; Mary Terriberry/Shutterstock.com: 48; Steven Wright/Shutterstock.com: 11; Spirit of America: 27 (top); U.S. Naval Academy Museum Collection: 60 (top).

Table of Contents

KEY ICONS TO LOOK FOR:

Words to Understand: These words with their easy-to-understand definitions will increase the reader's understanding of the text, while building vocabulary skills.

Sidebars: This boxed material within the main text allows readers to build knowledge, gain insights, explore possibilities, and broaden their perspectives by weaving together additional information to provide realistic and holistic perspectives.

Research Projects: Readers are pointed toward areas of further inquiry connected to each chapter. Suggestions are provided for projects that encourage deeper research and analysis.

Text-Dependent Questions: These questions send the reader back to the text for more careful attention to the evidence presented there.

Series Glossary of Key Terms: This back-of-the book glossary contains terminology used throughout this series. Words found here increase the reader's ability to read and comprehend higher-level books and articles in this field.

LET'S EXPLORE THE STATES

Atlantic: North Carolina, Virginia, West Virginia
Central Mississippi River Basin: Arkansas, Iowa, Missouri
East South-Central States: Kentucky, Tennessee
Eastern Great Lakes: Indiana, Michigan, Ohio
Gulf States: Alabama, Louisiana, Mississippi
Lower Atlantic: Florida, Georgia, South Carolina
Lower Plains: Kansas, Nebraska
Mid-Atlantic: Delaware, District of Columbia, Maryland
Non-Continental: Alaska, Hawaii
Northern New England: Maine, New Hampshire, Vermont
Northeast: New Jersey, New York, Pennsylvania
Northwest: Idaho, Oregon, Washington
Rocky Mountain: Colorado, Utah, Wyoming
Southern New England: Connecticut, Massachusetts, Rhode Island
Southwest: New Mexico, Oklahoma, Texas
U.S. Territories and Possessions
Upper Plains: Montana, North Dakota, South Dakota
The West: Arizona, California, Nevada
Western Great Lakes: Illinois, Minnesota, Wisconsin

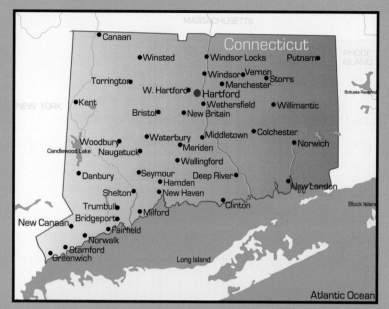

 ## Connecticut at a Glance

Area: 5,543 sq miles (14,356 sq km)[1].
48th-largest state
  Land: 4,824 sq miles (12,494 sq km)
  Water: 701 sq miles (1,816 sq km)
Highest elevation: Mt. Frissell,
  2,380 feet (725 m)
Lowest elevation: Long Island Sound
  (sea level)

Statehood: January 9, 1788
  (5th state)
Capital: Hartford

Population: 3,596,677
  (29th largest state)[2]

State nickname: Constitution State
State bird: American robin
State flower: Mountain Laurel

[1] *U.S. Census Bureau*
[2] *U.S. Census Bureau, 2014 estimate*

Connecticut

Connecticut, one of the 13 original colonies, got its name from the Algonquian word *quinnehtukqut*, which means "beside the long tidal river." English settlers kept this name but spelled it Connecticut. They used the name for both their colony and the Connecticut River, the most important river in New England. The Connecticut River flows across the middle of the state from north to south and empties into Long Island Sound.

Geography

Connecticut is the third-smallest state in the nation, covering only 5,543 square miles (14,356 sq km). It is bordered on the north by Massachusetts, on the west by New York, on the east by Rhode Island, and on the south by the waters of Long Island Sound. Connecticut can be divided into five geographic regions: Coastal Lowland, Eastern New England Upland, Connecticut Valley Lowland, Western New England Upland, and the Taconic Mountains.

The Coastal Lowland is a narrow strip of land that runs for 253 miles (407 km) along the Long Island Sound. Its main features are beaches and harbors.

Inland from the coast, the Eastern New England Upland is made up of many river valleys and low hills covered in forests. This region is part of a larger land formation that stretches across Connecticut, Massachusetts, and Maine.

Bordering the Eastern Upland to the west is the Connecticut Valley Lowland. The Connecticut River flows through this 30-mile-wide (48 km wide) area and empties into the Long Island Sound. Crops such as potatoes, corn, and *shade tobacco* grow in the fertile soil of this region.

The Western New England Upland covers the western one-third of the state. The soil is rocky and poor for farming, although some dairy cattle are raised here. Stone is quarried in this region and crushed into gravel for road building.

Words to Understand in This Chapter

comptroller—an elected official in the executive branch of the state of Connecticut who is responsible for paying the state's bills.

electoral votes—People vote in a popular election for the president, but the president is officially elected by electoral votes. Each state has votes equal to the total of its U.S. senators and Representatives.

median—middle.

poverty level—the level of income below which a person or family is declared poor by government standards.

ratify—to formally approve a document such as a treaty or the Constitution.

secretary of the state—In Connecticut, an elected official who is responsible for keeping the state's public documents in order.

shade tobacco—tobacco grown under netting that creates shade. The leaves are used as the outer wrapper for expensive cigars.

The Connecticut state capitol building can be seen through autumn foliage in Bushnell Park, Hartford.

The Taconic Mountains, which extend into New York, contain the highest hills in Connecticut, including the south slope of Mount Frissell, the highest point in the state. There are many opportunities for outdoor recreation in this area. The Appalachian Trail, a hiking trail that extends from Maine to Georgia, passes through the Taconic Mountains. The Housatonic River, popular with whitewater canoeists, flows through this region, then turns southeast and empties into Long Island Sound.

Connecticut has a four-season climate. Hartford, near the middle of the state, has an average high temperature of 34° Fahrenheit (1° Celsius) in

View of Lamentation Mountain State Park, near Berlin. The park is known for its hiking trails and unusual cliff formations.

January, and an high of 85°F (29°C) in July. Hartford receives about 44 inches (112 cm) of precipitation each year.

Coastal areas tend to have milder temperatures and more rainfall than Hartford. The western part of the state tends to be cooler and receives greater amounts of snow in the winter.

History

Before Europeans arrived, at least 16 Native American tribes lived in the region that is now Connecticut. These tribes belonged to a group called Algonquian. They were related by language and customs, but sometimes fought against each other. Three of the more important tribes were the powerful Pequot who lived along the coast; the Mohegan in eastern Connecticut; and the Quiripi, a group of small tribes that inhabited the western part of the state.

Adriaen Block was the first European to sail up the Connecticut River; in 1614, he claimed the river and surrounding territory for the Netherlands. Although the Dutch traded with the Algonquian natives, they didn't have much interest in building permanent settlements.

The first permanent settlers were English. During the mid-1630s, families from Puritan communities in Massachusetts began moving into

Connecticut. Some settlers established towns inland in the Connecticut River Valley near present-day Hartford. They called their settlement the Connecticut Colony. Others established the New Haven Colony near the coast.

At first, relations with the Algonquian tribes were peaceful, but that peace did not last. In 1637, an army of English settlers joined by warriors from the Narragansett and Mohegan tribes attacked the Pequot. They set fire to a large Pequot village and killed about 700 people. From that point, the power of the Pequot tribe was broken.

The early Puritan colonies in Massachusetts and Connecticut were theocracies, a form of government in which the religious leaders were also the political leaders. This changed in the Connecticut Colony with the arrival of Reverend Thomas Hooker. Hooker believed that men should have a voice in choosing their political leaders through elections. Under Hooker's influence, the Connecticut Colony adopted a set of eleven rules called the Fundamental Orders. They gave colonists a greater voice in their government.

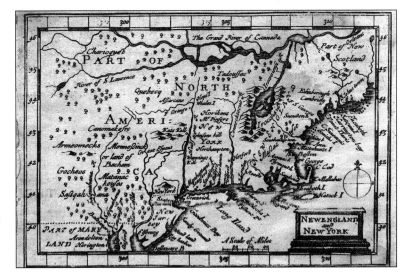

This map of England's North American colonies, created around 1675, shows several settlements in the Connecticut region, including New Haven and Hartford (which is spelled Herford on the map).

When the English arrived, the area where the Mystic River enters Long Island Sound was the site of a large Pequot village. After the Pequot war ended in 1638, the English established a settlement there. Today, Mystic Seaport is home to the largest maritime museum in the United States. It includes many old buildings, as well as sailing ships from the 19th century.

The Fundamental Orders are considered the first written Constitution in the colonies. The Orders did not create a democracy as we think of it today, however. The only people allowed to vote were adult white males who owned property and were Puritans. This excluded about 75 percent of the colonists.

As the population of Connecticut continued to grow, leaders worried that the British might restrict their form of self-government. In 1661, the colony sent John Winthrop Jr. to England to convince King Charles II to give Connecticut an official charter that would permit colonists to select their own political leaders and judges. Winthrop's mission was a success. In 1665, the New Haven Colony joined the Connecticut Colony, so that its citizens would have the same rights.

During the French and Indian War (1754–1763), Great Britain fought with France over the Ohio River Valley in North America. The war was expensive, and after it ended the British government began to impose taxes on the colonies to help pay for their defense. Protests against these taxes began in Massachusetts and spread throughout the 13 American colonies. In 1775, the Revolutionary War began.

Only four Revolutionary War battles were fought in Connecticut, but the colony contributed more than 30,000 men and thousands of dollars in money and supplies to support the Patriot cause. Connecticut also also produced a hero, a villain, and an interesting invention.

Nathan Hale, the hero, was a schoolteacher who served as a spy for the Continental army. He was captured in New York and hanged in 1776. Hale is remembered today for his last words: "I regret that I have but one life to give for my country."

Benedict Arnold, born in Norwich,

Benedict Arnold

went from being one of America's greatest heroes to its worst traitor. As a general in the Continental Army, he played a key role in the Battle of Saratoga in

The British executed Nathan Hale as a spy in 1776.

October 1777, one of the most important American victories. However, when Arnold didn't get a promotion that he wanted, he became angry. In 1780, he secretly offered to turn over the American fort at West Point to the British. The plot was uncovered, and Arnold fled to Britain. He returned in

 Did You Know?

The Hartford Courant, a newspaper established in 1764, is the oldest American newspaper that has been continuously published.

Noah Webster (1748–1843), born in West Hartford, wanted the United States to be united by language. During the 1780s he published A Grammatical Institute of the English Language, *popularly called the "blue-backed speller." It standardized spelling and pronunciation of words for school children. Later he published the* American Dictionary of the English Language *(1828). He added American words like "skunk" and "squash" and used American, not British spellings for words like "color."*

1781, this time leading British troops on a raid of the Connecticut seaport at New London. That battle was bloody and controversial, as Arnold's men massacred 150 members of Connecticut's militia who were trying to surrender. After the war ended, Arnold spent the rest of his life in Canada and London.

David Bushnell produced the most unusual invention of the Revolution. In 1775, he built the first submarine. The one-man vessel, called the *Turtle*, carried a bomb full of gunpowder that Bushnell thought could be attached to the hull of an enemy ship and detonated. The *Turtle* tried but failed to blow up British ships in the harbors at Boston and New York. However, some of Bushnell's designs were incorporated into later submarines. Today, the U.S. Navy's main submarine base is located on the Thames River at Groton.

After the Revolutionary War ended in victory for the Patriots in 1783, the states had to find a way to work together. Their first attempt to form a united government, under the Articles of Confederation, was a failure. In 1787,

Roger Sherman was one of three delegates sent to represent Connecticut at a convention in Philadelphia to create a national government.

At the convention, there was a dispute about how the states would be represented in the national legislature, called Congress. Large states wanted the number of legislators to be a percentage of each state's population. This would give the more populous states more representatives. Smaller states wanted every state to have the same number of representatives, so that their concerns would be heard.

Sherman came up with a solution called the Connecticut Compromise. Congress would include two legislative bodies. The number of legislators in the House of Representatives would be based on each state's population. In the Senate, each state would have two representatives, regardless of population size. This ended the dispute. On January 9, 1788, Connecticut became the fifth state to *ratify* the U.S. Constitution.

Connecticut has a limited amount of good farmland, so during the

Roger Sherman was an important political leader in early America. He helped to write the Declaration of Independence, and played a key role in passage of the U.S. Constitution.

Industrial Revolution in the first half of the 19th century the state became known as a center of manufacturing. Eli Whitney, born in Massachusetts, attended Yale University and established a factory near New Haven that manufactured firearms. Other well-known firearms companies were also founded in Connecticut, including Colt, Winchester, and Smith & Wesson. Factories in Connecticut also made clocks, ships, and tools.

Like other New England states, residents of Connecticut generally opposed slavery, although black men did not gain full citizenship until 1870. When the country was threatened by civil war, Connecticut residents wanted to hold the Union

Famous People from Connecticut

In 1817, after traveling to England and France to learn sign language, Thomas Gallaudet (1787–1851), founded the first school for the deaf in Hartford. His son, Edward (1837–1917), carried on the tradition by establishing Gallaudet University in Washington, D. C. It is the first American college for the deaf.

Harriet Beecher Stowe

Samuel Colt

Harriett Beecher Stowe (1811–1896) found fame in 1852 as the author of the anti-slavery novel *Uncle Tom's Cabin*. The book was translated into over 60 languages. It showed the dreadful condition of slaves who were treated like property rather than humans. Stowe said, "I wrote what I wrote because as a woman, as a mother, I was oppressed and broken-hearted with the sorrows and injustice I saw."

Samuel Colt (1814–1862) of Hartford invented the first revolver, a gun that could fire multiple shots without reloading. He established a factory in Hartford that used interchangeable parts and an assembly line to produce guns more cheaply and efficiently. During the Civil War, he sold guns to both the North and the South.

Phineas Taylor (P.T.) Barnum (1810–1891) of Bethel was one of the world's greatest showmen. Specializing in hoaxes and human curiosities, Barnum put together a highly successful traveling show called The Greatest Show on Earth. After his death, the show merged with similar shows and lives on today as Ringling Bros. Barnum & Bailey Circus.

A modern author born in Hartford, Stephenie Meyer (b. 1973) has had great success with the four-book young adult Twilight series. The books, which feature a romance between a vampire and a human, have sold millions of copies and been made into highly successful movies.

Stephenie Meyer

together. During the American Civil War arrived (1861–1865), about 55,000 men volunteered to fight. Notable leaders from Connecticut included Admiral Andrew Hull Foote, who commanded Union gunboats in several important victories in the western theatre of the war.

During the decades after the Civil War ended, Connecticut received a new influx of immigrants from Ireland, Germany, and Italy. Many of these immigrants went to work in new factories located along the coast, or in inland towns that were served by a growing railroad system.

The boom years for Connecticut manufacturing ended in 1929 when the nation went into the Great Depression. Factories closed and many people were unemployed. Manufacturing did not pick up again until the United States entered World War II in 1941. During the war, factories in Connecticut produced ships, submarines, helicopters, and airplane parts for the U.S. military. Today, the defense industry remains a vital part of Connecticut's economy.

During the 1960s, Connecticut saw its share of the racial tension that accompanied the Civil Rights Movement. Riots occurred in cities such as Hartford, New Haven, and Waterbury. School systems in some cities were forced by the federal government to desegregate. Changes came slowly, but in 1987, Carrie Saxon Perry became mayor of Hartford, the first African-American woman elected mayor of a major city. Today Connecticut's minority communities continue to make their voices heard through the ballot box.

Government

Connecticut had the first constitution in the American colonies, the Fundamental Orders. Today, the state government operates under a newer constitution that was ratified in 1965.

State government is divided into three branches: executive, legislative, and judicial. The executive branch consists of the governor, lieutenant governor, *secretary of the state*, treasurer, *comptroller*, and attorney general. These positions are filled by a

(Top) The Connecticut State Capitol building houses the state's General Assembly, as well as the governor's office. Dannel P. Malloy (below) was elected governor in 2010, and was re-elected in 2014.

statewide election every four years.

The General Assembly is the legislative branch of the government. It consists of two legislative bodies, or "houses." The Connecticut Senate has 36 members, while the House of Representatives has 151 members. Each member represents a specific geographic district. Both senators and representatives are elected for two-year terms. For a bill to become law, it must be passed by both houses of the General Assembly and be signed by the governor.

In the judicial branch, most court cases are settled in district courts or superior courts. Judges for these courts are elected by the General Assembly. Decisions made by these courts can be taken to the Appellate Court for review and finally to the Supreme Court. Supreme Court judges are nominated by the governor but must be approved by the General Assembly. Unlike the United States Supreme Court where justices serve for life, justices on the Connecticut Supreme Court serve eight-year terms.

Connecticut sends two senators and five representatives to Washington D.C. to represent the state in Congress. This gives the state seven *electoral votes* in presidential elections.

The Economy

In colonial times, Connecticut was an agricultural state. Today with only 4,200 farms, agriculture plays a small role in the economy. Tobacco and hay are the state's two largest crops.

Insurance and financial services drive much of Connecticut's economy. Connecticut ranked first in the nation in insurance employment in 2012. About 3 percent of the state's workers were employed in this field. Aetna, UnitedHealthcare, and Travelers are large insurance companies with head-quarters in the Hartford area.

The defense industry also con-tributes to Connecticut's economy. Overall, more than 1,100 Connecticut firms, employing over 100,000 people, are involved in manufacturing and repairing military equipment.

One of these companies is the Electric Boat Corporation, which has been building submarines for the U.S. Navy for more than 100 years. It built the first nuclear submarine in 1954, and has a manufacturing and repair facility at the shipyard in Groton.

The Sikorsky Aircraft Corporation, founded by Russian immigrant Igor Sikorsky, is headquartered in Stratford. The company produced the first working helicopter in 1939. Today it manufactures many different types of helicopters, including the Black Hawk military helicopter.

Hartford is home to the head-quarters of many major insur-ance companies, including Travelers, Aetna, The Hartford, The Phoenix Companies, UnitedHealthcare, and Hartford Steam Boiler. Founded in 1635, it is one of the oldest cities in the United States, and is Connecticut's fourth-largest city.

Yale University, founded in 1701, is one of the most respected institutions of higher learning in North America. The statue on the campus here represents Theodore Dwight Woolsey, who served as president of the college from 1846 to 1871.

Connecticut is a state with very rich and very poor areas. The *median* household income in Connecticut in 2014 was about $70,000, which is more than $16,000 higher than the national average. However, 10 percent of residents have incomes below the *poverty* level.

The People

In the census of 1800, Connecticut had 251,002 residents. By 2014, that number had grown to almost 3.6 million, making Connecticut the 29th most populous state in the nation.

Immigration has contributed to Connecticut's population growth. According to the U.S. Census Bureau, about 14 percent of the state's residents were born in a foreign country, while 21 percent speak a language other than English at home. These percentages are slightly higher than the average for the United States as a whole.

Due to Connecticut's history, around 19 percent of the population claims Italian heritage, while 18 percent is of Irish descent. The Census Bureau reports 82 percent of the state's population self-identify as white. However, this figure includes 14 percent who also identify as Hispanic or Latino. African Americans make up 11 percent of the population.

Roman Catholicism is the most popular religion in Connecticut, with 36 percent of residents adhering to its beliefs. About 13 percent of Connecticut residents belong to other Christian churches, while 2 percent practice other religions, including Judaism and Islam.

Residents of Connecticut are better educated than the nation as a whole. According to Census data, 89 percent have high school diplomas while 36 percent have earned a bachelor's degree or higher. (The national averages are 85.7 percent and 28.5 percent, respectively.)

Major Cities

The most densely populated area of Connecticut is the coastal strip that borders the southern part of the Long Island Sound. The state's two largest cities, Bridgeport and New Haven, are found here.

Bridgeport is home to the Barnum Museum, which celebrates the accomplishments of 19th century showman P.T. Barnum. The unusual building, built in 1893 with funds provided by Barnum himself, is on the National Register of Historic Places. Although best known as an entertainer, Barnum served four terms in the Connecticut legislature, and was also elected mayor of Bridgeport in 1875.

Bridgeport was a thriving manufacturing town until the 1970s when factories began closing and many residents moved to the suburbs. After a difficult period, the city declared bankruptcy in 1991. Redevelopment programs have helped Bridgeport recover. Today many residents attracted by lower housing costs work in New York City and commute from Bridgeport by train.

Many large corporations have offices in Stamford, the state's third-largest city.

worked hard to shed its image as a dangerous place. Yale University, the third-oldest university in the United States, is the city's largest employer.

Hartford, the capital, is known as the "Insurance Capital of the World" because of the many insurance companies headquartered there. Mark Twain, author of *The Adventures of Tom Sawyer*, lived in Hartford for 17 years. His house, now a National Historic Landmark, is open to the public.

Like Bridgeport, *New Haven* suffered a decline beginning in the 1960s as manufacturing jobs left the city. By the late 1990s, the violent crime rate in some neighborhoods was dangerously high. Since then, the city has

Although some Connecticut cities have experienced urban decay, many of the state's smaller towns, such as *Greenwich, New Canaan, Westport*, and *Lyme* are among the wealthiest in southern New England.

Further Reading

Alef, Daniel. *Igor I. Sikorsky: Big Dreams, Big Planes, and the Rise of Helicopters.* Santa Barbara, Calif.: Titans of Fortune Publishing, 2011.

Burgan, Michael and Stephanie Fitzgerald. *Connecticut.* New York: Marshall Cavendish Benchmark, 2011.

Fleming, Candace. *The Great and Only Barnum: The Tremendous, Stupendous Life of Showman P.T. Barnum.* New York: Schwartz & Wade Books, 2009.

Lefkowits, Arnold. *Bushnell's Submarine.* New York: Scholastic Nonfiction, 2006.

Internet Resources

http://www.kids.ct.gov/kids/site/default.asp

ConneCT Kids is the official state web site for children.

http://www.ctvisit.com/#27477

The official site of the Connecticut Office of Tourism

http://emuseum.chs.org:8080/emuseum

Connecticut Historical Society Museum and Library allows electronic searches of documents, people, and objects.

 # Text-Dependent Questions

1. What happened to the Native Americans living in Connecticut when Europeans arrived?
2. Why were the Fundamental Orders important?
3. What is the Connecticut Compromise?

 # Research Project

Research one of the following people and write a one-page essay explaining why they were important to Connecticut: Roger Sherman, Igor Sikorski, Samuel Colt, or Benedict Arnold.

Fall foliage covers the Litchfield Hills in northwestern Connecticut.

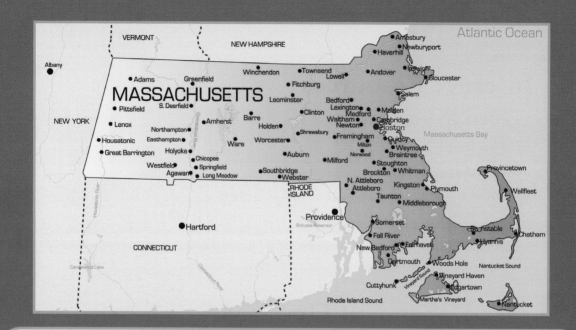

Massachusetts at a Glance

Area: 10,554 sq miles (27,335 sq km)[1]
   (44th largest state)
   Land: 7,800 sq mi (20,201 sq km)
   Water: 2,754 sq mi (7,133 sq km)
Highest elevation: Mount Greylock,
   3,487 feet (1,064 m)
Lowest elevation: Atlantic Ocean,
   sea level

Statehood: February 6, 1788
   (2nd state)
Capital: Boston

Population: 6,745,408
   (14th largest state)[2]

State nickname: Bay State
State bird: Black-capped Chickadee
State flower: Mayflower

[1] *U.S. Census Bureau*
[2] *U.S. Census Bureau, 2014 estimate*

Massachusetts

Massachusetts is sometimes called the Cradle of Liberty because of the important role the Massachusetts colony played during the American Revolution. It could also be called the Cradle of Public Education, as a 1647 law required all towns with 50 or more families to provide a free elementary education to all children. The state was also the first to require all children to attend school. Frederick Douglass, an escaped slave who settled in New Bedford, once wrote that in Massachusetts, "the black man's children attended public schools with the white man's children, and apparently without objection from any quarter."

Geography

In colonial times, Massachusetts included parts of New Hampshire and Maine and stretched from the Atlantic to the Pacific Ocean. Today, Massachusetts covers 10,544 square miles (27,335 sq km). It is the largest state in southern New England, but only the forty-fourth largest in the nation.

Massachusetts is bordered on the north by Vermont and New Hampshire and on the south by Connecticut and Rhode Island. New York forms its western boundary, and the Atlantic Ocean lies to the east, giving Massachusetts 192 miles (309 km) of coastline. The state measures roughly 185 miles (298 km) from east to west and 110 miles (177 km) from north to south. It contains six major geographic regions: Costal Lowland, Eastern New England Upland, Connecticut Valley Lowland, Western New England Upland, Berkshire Valley, and Taconic Mountains.

The Coastal Lowland extends from the Atlantic Ocean inland for about 50 miles (81 km). The state's nickname, the Bay State, comes from three prominent bays along the Atlantic coast: Massachusetts Bay, Cape Cod Bay, and Buzzards Bay. Off the coast of Cape Cod are the islands of Martha's Vineyard and Nantucket. Cranberry farming and tourism are

Words to Understand in This Chapter

artist colony—a place, usually in a rural area, where writers, artists, or other creative people go to spend several weeks working on their art free of the pressures of daily life.

auditor—an unbiased person who examines the financial health of an organization.

Commonwealth—meaning "for the common good," in the United States it is the same as a state. Massachusetts, Pennsylvania, Virginia, and Kentucky all identify themselves as commonwealths.

nor'easter—a strong storm with winds that blow from the northeast.

nursery plants—plants usually started in greenhouses and sold to landscapers and gardeners.

secede—to withdraw; specifically for a state to leave the United States.

West Indies—Islands in the Caribbean between the United States and South America.

View of the Berkshire Mountains in autumn.

important industries along the coast. Boston is located on the innermost part of Massachusetts Bay. The Merrimack River is in the northern part of the Coastal Lowland, and the Taunton River is in the south.

The Eastern New England Upland lies west of the Coastal Lowland. Worcester, the second-largest city in the state, is located at its eastern edge. The rocky hills of the Eastern Upland extend between 40 to 60 miles (64 to 96 km) to the west. The hills slope down to the west where they meet the Connecticut Valley Lowlands. This region is home to many small fruit, vegetable, and dairy farms.

The Connecticut Valley Lowland stretches in a narrow band no more than 20 miles (32 km) wide along the Connecticut River. The soil here is some of the most fertile in New

Annisquam Light at Gloucester, a city on Cape Ann. Gloucester is an important center of the fishing industry in Massachusetts.

This Veterans War Memorial tower is located at the top of Mount Greylock, the highest point in Massachusetts. Parts of five states can be seen from this mountain in the Taconic range.

The Western New England Upland extends 20 to 30 miles (32 to 48 km) west of the Connecticut Valley. Here mountains reach elevations of 3,000 feet (915 m). The highest peak in Massachusetts, Mount Greylock, is in this region. The Western Upland, along with the Berkshire Valley, a low strip of land 10 miles (16 km) wide that separates the Berkshire Hills from the Taconic Mountains to the west, is known for its universities, *artist colonies*, and outdoor recreation opportunities. The Hoosic and Hoosatonic Rivers are formed by streams that originate in the Berkeley Hills.

The lightly populated Taconic Mountains form a band less than six miles (10 km) wide. This marks the border between Massachusetts and New York.

Massachusetts has warm, humid summers and cold winters. The average high temperature in Boston in January is 36°F (2°C), while the average high in July is 81°F (27°C). Boston gets almost 44 inches (112 cm) of snow and another 40 inches

England. Farmers raise apples and vegetables, as well as plants and shrubs for the landscaping industry. Springfield, the third-largest city in Massachusetts, is located at the southern end of the Connecticut Valley.

(102 cm) of rain each year. In the western part of the state where elevations are higher, snowfall amounts are greater.

Hurricanes from the Atlantic sometimes hit the state, especially Cape Cod. In addition, strong winter storms known as *nor'easters* can push water from the oceans and bays inland to cause serious coastal flooding.

History

Native Americans known as the Algonquian lived in what is now Massachusetts for 3,000 years before Europeans arrived. The Algonquian peoples formed separate tribes but were linked by language and customs. Tribes in Massachusetts included the Pennacook, Nauset, Wampanoag, Nipmuc, Mohican, and Pocumtuc.

Europeans visited New England long before they settled there. English explorer Bartholomew Gosnold landed in Massachusetts in 1602. He was so impressed with the fish he caught that he named the fishing area Cape Cod Bay. None of the explorers who visited the area stayed, but they inad-

Nor'easters are strong storms that hit the upper Atlantic coast, especially New England and Canada. These storms are often accompanied by heavy rain or blizzard-like snow.

vertently exposed the native people to deadly diseases for which they had no resistance. These reduced the Native American population, from 30,000 to about 7,000.

The first Europeans to build a permanent settlement in Massachusetts were Protestants who disagreed with the teaching of the Church of England and were punished for their beliefs. These people saw the voyage to the New World as a pilgrimage to find religious freedom, which is why we now call them Pilgrims.

Plymouth Rock marks the spot where the Pilgrims landed in North America in 1620. Today, to keep tourists from chiseling off pieces of the rock, it is protected in a granite shelter.

A group of 102 Pilgrims left Europe on the ship *Mayflower*, intending to sail to Virginia, where an English settlement had been established in 1607. They were blown off course by Atlantic storms. On November 21, 1620, after sailing for 65 days, they landed at the tip of Cape Cod near present-day Provincetown. Three weeks later, they sailed across Cape Cod Bay and founded a permanent colony at Plymouth.

The Pilgrims were unprepared for Massachusetts's harsh winter. "There died sometimes two or three a day" wrote William Bradford, their leader. By spring, half the colonists were dead. Things improved when a friendly Native American showed the Pilgrims how to grow corn. By autumn Bradford wrote, they had "all good things in plenty." After the harvest, the Pilgrims organized a feast, the first Thanksgiving, attended by many Native Americans.

Ten years later in 1630, the Puritans, another English group seeking religious freedom, arrived to start their own colony, the Massachusetts Bay Colony. Under the leadership of John Winthrop, they settled first in Salem, then moved to what would become Boston.

Although the Puritans wanted freedom to practice their religion as they wished, they were intolerant of the beliefs of others. Anyone who did not agree with their strict religious views or way of life was driven out of the colony. This included Roger Williams and Anne Hutchinson, who left in the 1630s to establish a colony in Rhode Island. Another was John Wheelwright, who established a colony at Exeter, New Hampshire in 1638. That same year, Thomas Hooker, a prominent Puritan minister, helped to found the Connecticut Colony.

Both the Plymouth Colony and the Massachusetts Bay Colony prospered over the following decades. In 1691 King William of England decided to combine the two colonies, as well as other North American territories, to create the Province of Massachusetts.

New England's location near the French colonies in Canada led to numerous conflicts in North America during the 17th and 18th centuries. The largest of these was the French and Indian War, which began in 1754. At the conclusion of that conflict in 1763, the British parliament began taxing American colonists to offset the cost of their defense. Citizens in Massachusetts and elsewhere rebelled with the cry "no taxation without rep-

The Pilgrims and the Puritans were two distinctly different groups. The Pilgrims were dissenters who wanted to separate themselves completely from the Church of England. The Puritans wanted to reform, or "purify," the the Church of England. They established their colony in New England in 1630 because the king of England, Charles I, opposed their reform attempts.

resentation." Boston was at the heart of colonial opposition to the new taxes.

In December of 1773, Patriots in Boston boarded a British ship and dumped 342 chests of tea into the harbor to protest the tax. The British responded to this act of defiance, known as the Boston Tea Party, by closing Boston Harbor in 1774, and sending soldiers to Massachusetts.

The first shots of the Revolutionary War were fired in April 1775, when British troops marched on Lexington and Concord, two towns just outside Boston. They were looking for military supplies hidden by the colonists. Paul Revere and other Patriots rode through the night to warn people that the British were coming. Members of the local militia, called Minutemen, responded. At Lexington, the British fired on the Minutemen, killing eight Americans. However, as the British Army retreated back to Boston, the American militia followed and attacked constantly. Many British soldiers were killed.

After this, American soldiers surrounded the city to prevent the British Army from marching out. At the Battle of Bunker Hill in June 1775, a British frontal assault on the Americans resulted in high casualties, but failed to break the siege. In March 1776, Henry Knox brought cannons captured at Fort Ticonderoga to George Washington, who placed them on hills around the city. This forced the British to sail away from Boston.

When the War for Independence ended in 1783, the 13 colonies were working together under a system of government called the Articles of Confederation. However, this system did not give the national government much power to raise taxes, enforce

 Did You Know?

Patriot's Day, the third Monday in April, is a legal holiday in Massachusetts. It commemorates the Battles of Lexington and Concord. The Boston Marathon, the world's oldest annual marathon, is always held on Patriot's Day.

American soldiers on Breed's Hill near Boston await a frontal assault by the British Army. The June 1775 clash is known as the Battle of Bunker Hill for a nearby high point that was also fortified by the Continental Army. It ended with the British holding the hills, but at a high cost in casualties.

laws, or respond to a crisis. Such a crisis occurred in Massachusetts during 1786, when farmers led by Daniel Shays, a Revolutionary War veteran, took over the courthouse in Northampton. Due to the difficulty in ending Shays's Rebellion, a convention was held the next year in Philadelphia to create a new system of national government. On February 6, 1788, Massachusetts became the sixth state to ratify the U.S. Constitution.

Massachusetts was an important center of trade, and ships from Boston sailed for Europe, China, and the *West Indies*. This changed in 1807 when France and Great Britain were at war. Each country's navy blockaded the other's ports. This prevented American ships from unloading or picking up cargo, and caused economic problems throughout New England.

That blockade ended in 1809, but in 1812, the United States went to war with Great Britain and a new blockade began. The War of 1812 was so unpopular that some people in Massachusetts wanted to *secede*, or break away, from the Union. After the war ended, in 1820 the northern part of Massachusetts became a separate state, Maine.

The blockades of the early 19th century, as well as the Industrial Revolution, changed Massachusetts. The country began to manufacture more of its own goods, rather than importing finished products from Europe. Francis Cabot Lowell opened a textile factory powered by water from the Charles River. Soon, other factories followed. Within 20 years, Massachusetts was a manufacturing center. One of the largest factories was in a city named for Lowell, where the Merrimac River dropped 32 feet (10 m). This provided enough water-power to run a mill that employed nearly 10,000 people.

Factory work attracted new immigrants and young women who left farms for what they hoped would be a better life. Conditions in the mills were horrid, however. The hours were long, the pay low, and the machines noisy, and dangerous. Children as young as seven often worked twelve-hour days. Conditions were so bad that in 1836, Massachusetts became the first state to pass laws limiting child labor. Today the mills are part of the Lowell National Historic Park.

At roughly the same time, Bay Staters turned their attention to other

Visitors listen as a park ranger explains the history of cloth production at the Boott Cotton Mill Museum in Lowell, which is run by the National Park Service.

Dorothea Dix

social problems. Dorothea Dix worked to improve treatment of prisoners and the mentally ill. Horace Mann pushed to standardize the quality of teacher training and free public education by setting up the first state board of education. Lucy Stone and Susan B. Anthony spoke out for women's rights. And although Massachusetts had out-

Horace Mann

lawed slavery in 1780, William Lloyd Garrison stirred up public support for the national abolition of slavery with his newspaper, the *Liberator*.

The fight against slavery eventually led to the American Civil War (1861–1865). Throughout the conflict, Massachusetts factories churned out uniforms, shoes, and guns for the Union army. Massachusetts also contributed about

William Lloyd Garrison

150,000 men to the fight. The 54th Massachusetts Volunteer Infantry Regiment was the first Civil War unit of black soldiers to be raised in the North. They fought bravely at Fort Wagner in South Carolina, losing many men.

Massachusetts was called on again to send men to fight in World War I (1914–1918). About 200,000 of them answered the call. Massachusetts factories supported the war effort by manufacturing guns and war supplies.

Following the end of World War I, thousands of European immigrants poured into Massachusetts. The 1920 census showed that almost 70 percent

This painting depicts the death of Colonel Robert Gould Shaw during the 54th Massachusetts Regiment's attack on Fort Wagner, South Carolina, in July 1863.

Did You Know?

Boston built the first subway system in America. It opened on September 1, 1897, three years before New York's subway. The tunnels were dug by hand with picks and shovels. During the digging, workers found more than 900 unmarked graves.

of the state's residents were either foreign born or children of foreign-born parents. These immigrants provided an cheap labor for Massachusetts factories.

The good economic times ended in 1929, when the stock market crashed. During the Great Depression, factories closed and jobs were scarce. At the height of the Depression, almost one-third of adult men in Massachusetts were unemployed. Job growth did not pick up again until after the United States entered World War II in 1941. Then, once again, Massachusetts's factories worked overtime to produce the materials needed to wage war.

After the war ended, however, companies began closing their factories in Massachusetts and moving to the South, where they could produce goods more cheaply. Over time the state transitioned toward an economy based on high technology, financial services, and tourism.

During the 1980s, a major construction project to reroute traffic began in Boston. Known as the "Big Dig," the project relocated a major interstate highway into a tunnel under the city. After many problems and delays, the project was completed in 2007 at a cost of nearly $15 billion.

Government

The *Commonwealth* of Massachusetts is governed from the State House in Boston. The state constitution, written by John Adams, was adopted in 1788. It is the oldest state constitution still in use today.

The government of Massachusetts consists of three branches: executive, legislative, and judicial. The executive branch is headed by the governor. Among the governor's duties are preparing the state budget, appointing judges, and approving (or rejecting) laws passed by the legislative branch. Other officials of the executive branch include the lieutenant governor, attorney general, treasurer, *auditor*, and secretary of state, each of whom are elected to four year terms in office.

The legislative branch is called the Court General. It has two divisions, the Senate, with 40 members, and the House of Representatives with 160 members. The state legislature is responsible for proposing and passing laws, which the governor may accept or veto. Legislators are elected every two years.

The judicial branch enforces and interprets the laws. Cases are initially heard in local district courts or in superior courts. Decisions made in

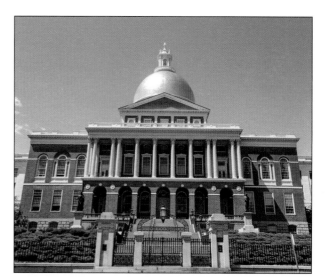

The state legislature meets in the historic Massachusetts State House, in the Beacon Hill neighborhood of Boston. The building was constructed in 1798, with major expansions in 1895 and 1917.

Deval Patrick served as governor of Massachusetts from 2007 until 2015.

these courts can be reviewed by appellate courts. The state's Supreme Court has the final word on judicial decisions. The governor appoints judges, who must be confirmed by an eight-member judicial council.

Bay Staters send two senators and nine representatives to Washington, D.C., to represent Massachusetts in Congress. This gives the state 11 electoral votes in presidential elections.

Massachusetts Families in Politics

Massachusetts has produced two families in which several members have played an important role in American political history: the Adams family and the Kennedy family.

John Adams (1735–1826) was one of the most important American leaders during the War for Independence. He helped write the Declaration of Independence and later served as George Washington's vice president. He was the second president of the United States, serving from 1796 to 1800. His second cousin, Samuel Adams (1722–1803), encouraged American independence by setting up a committee of correspondence, which allowed Patriot leaders in the thirteen colonies to keep in touch with one another before the War for Independence began. John Adams's son, John Quincy Adams (1767–1848), was the sixth president of the United States, serving from 1824 to 1828. After leaving the White House, John Quincy Adams served 17 years in Congress as a representative for Massachusetts, where he became known for his stance against slavery.

John F. Kennedy (1917–1963) was the 35th president of the United States, serving from 1961 until he was assassinated in November 1963. His brother, Edward "Ted" Kennedy (1932–2009) represented Massachusetts in the U.S. Senate for 47 years. Another brother, Robert "Bobby" Kennedy (1925–1968), was a nationally known political figure who was assassinated while running for president in June 1968.

Several of their descendants have continued the Kennedy legacy in national politics. Ted Kennedy's son Patrick (b. 1967) represented Rhode Island in Congress from 1995 to 2011. John Kennedy's daughter Caroline (b. 1957) was appointed in 2013 to serve as U.S. Ambassador to Japan.

The Kennedy family, circa 1931.

The Economy

During colonial times, Massachusetts built a strong economy on fishing and trade. In the early 1800s, the state began to become industrialized. It soon became known for factories that produced textiles, shoes, tools, armaments, and other items.

Today, the Massachusetts economy has become very diverse. The state has a well-educated population, as well as a large number of colleges and universities, and these have been leveraged to make Massachusetts a leader in education, medical research, and biotechnology. Financial services provide more than 180,000 jobs, mainly in the Boston area.

Agriculture is only a small part of the Massachusetts economy. The state has only 7,700 farms, more than 80 percent of which are family owned. The main agricultural products are **nursery plants**, cranberries, dairy products, and apples. Fishing and fish farming are also important industries. The state has few mineral resources.

Tourism has become the dominant service industry in Massachusetts. In

Since 2000, the New England Patriots have been one of the most successful NFL teams. The Patriots play their home games in Foxborough, a suburb of Boston.

2014, the state's department of tourism reported that more than 24 million people visited Massachusetts, spending more than $18.5 billion. Tourism supports about 130,000 jobs in the state.

According to the U.S. Census Bureau, the median household income in Massachusetts is $66,658, which is more than $13,000 higher than the national average. Eleven percent of the state's residents have incomes

Famous People from Massachusetts

Calvin Coolidge (1872–1933) was governor of Massachusetts from 1919 to 1921. He served as vice president to Warren G. Harding from 1921 until Harding's death in 1923, when he assumed the presidency. He was elected to a full term as president in 1924. Other Bay Staters who served as U.S. president include John Adams, John Quincy Adams, and John F. Kennedy. George H.W. Bush, president from 1989 to 1993, was born in Milton in 1924.

Calvin Coolidge

One of the most productive men of the 18th century, Benjamin Franklin (1706–1790), was born in Boston. Franklin was a printer, author, inventor, diplomat, statesman, scientist, and philosopher.

Clara Barton (1821–1912), born in North Oxford, was a nurse who founded the American Red Cross in 1881.

Theodore Seuss Geisel (1904–1991), better known as Dr. Seuss, had his first book, *And to Think That I Saw It on Mulberry Street*, rejected 27 times before it was published. He later went on to publish 44 children's books, the most famous of which is *The Cat in the Hat*.

Cambridge-born actor and screenwriter Matt Damon (b. 1970) has starred in films such as *Saving Private Ryan* and *Ocean's Eleven*. Damon and his childhood friend Ben Affleck (b. 1972), who grew up in Falmouth and Cambridge, won an Oscar for writing the 1998 film *Good Will Hunting*. Since then Affleck has appeared in many films, and has also been praised for his work as a movie director.

Another actor, Boston-born Leonard Nimoy (b. 1931), is known throughout the world as Dr. Spock of *Star Trek*. Nimoy is also a photographer and a poet.

Matt Damon (left) and Ben Affleck (right) celebrate their Oscar win with Good Will Hunting *costar Robin Williams.*

below the poverty level.

The People

In the census of 1800, Massachusetts had 422,845 residents. By 2014, that number had grown to over 6.7 million. Massachusetts is the 14th most populous state, but it is third in population density, with an average of 840 people per square mile.

Women in the state outnumber men by about 200,000. About 15 percent of the population was born in a foreign country, and 22 percent speak a language other than English at home. These percentages are slightly higher than the average for the United States.

In 2014, 84 percent of the population self-identified as white; this figure included about 10 percent who identified as Hispanic or Latino. Blacks made up 8 percent of the population, and Asians 6 percent.

Massachusetts residents tend to actively practice religion more than people in the nation as a whole. About 46 percent of the state's residents are Roman Catholic, roughly 9 percent

The Boston Red Sox play in Fenway Park, one of the oldest major league baseball stadiums. The park is known for its high leftfield wall, nicknamed the "Green Monster." The Red Sox won the World Series in 2004, 2007, and 2013.

belong to other Christian churches, and about 2 percent follow other religions.

Compared to the rest of the country, Bay Staters are well educated. Eighty-nine percent have graduated from high school and 39 percent have earned a bachelor's degree or higher. This reflects Massachusetts's long history of supporting public education, as well as the large number of colleges and universities in the state.

Tourists often rub the left shoe of the John Harvard statue on the campus of Harvard University, believing it will bring them luck. Harvard, the first college in North America, is among the world's most elite institutions of higher learning.

Major Cities

Boston, the capital of Massachusetts, is the largest city in New England. The city of Boston itself is fairly small, covering only 48 square miles (124 sq km), but including the towns that surround it, the Boston metropolitan area has a population of 4.5 million. This makes it the tenth-largest metropolitan area in the United States.

Boston was a major American city during the American Revolution. The Freedom Trail, a 2.5-mile (4 km) walking tour of 16 historic landmarks, includes Old North Church, where lanterns were hung to signal the route of the British invasion in 1775; Paul Revere's house; and the USS *Constitution*, the warship known as "Old Ironsides" for its exploits during the War of 1812.

Worcester is the second-largest city in Massachusetts. It is located near the center of the state. Through the early 1950s, Worcester was a busy manufacturing center. Gradually, companies moved their factories to less expensive areas in the South and West, and Worcester fell into decline. However, urban redevelopment during the early 2000s brought new jobs to the city. By 2013, 38 percent of all

This unusual round stone barn was built in Hancock in 1826.

The Central Artery/Tunnel Project, known informally as the "Big Dig," changed the face of Boston by rerouting Interstate 93 into a tunnel beneath the city.

jobs in Worcester were in education or the medical field. The city is home to nine colleges and universities, including the University of Massachusetts Medical School and Tufts Cummings School of Veterinary Medicine.

Located on the Connecticut River,

Springfield is the third-largest city in Massachusetts. Springfield is well known for its production of firearms. The Springfield Armory produced rifles for the U.S. Army for nearly 200 years, until it closed in 1968. Today, the Armory is a National Historic Site.

The Naismith Memorial Basketball Hall of Fame is located in Springfield. It is named for Dr. James Naismith, who invented the sport of basketball while teaching a gym class at the YMCA International Training School (now Springfield College) in 1891.

Smith & Wesson, a small arms manufacturer, was established in Springfield in 1852 and still has its headquarters there. Springfield is also the headquarters of Merriam-Webster, the publisher of dictionaries.

Many of the smaller towns in western Massachusetts are home to well-known colleges and universities. These towns include ***Amherst, Great Barrington, North Adams***, and ***South Hadley***.

Further Reading

Fraustino, Lisa Rowe. *I Walk in Dread: The Diary of Deliverance Trembley, Witness to the Salem Witch Trials.* New York: Scholastic, 2004.

Hinman, Bonnie. *The Massachusetts Bay Colony: The Puritans Arrive from England.* Hockessin, Del.: Mitchell Lane Publishers, 2007.

Jerome, Kate Boehm. *Boston and The State of Massachusetts: Cool Stuff Every Kid Should Know.* Charleston, S.C.: Arcadia Publishing, 2011.

Miller, Brandon Marie. *Benjamin Franklin, American Genius: His Life and Ideas with 21 Activities.* Chicago: Chicago Review Press, 2010.

Trueit, Trudi Strain. *Massachusetts.* New York: Children's Press, 2008.

Internet Resources

http://www.geo.umass.edu/faculty/wilkie/Wilkie/maps.html

A historical atlas of Massachusetts, with maps showing geographic regions, the site of pre-European native settlements, the spread of European settlements, population distribution across time, and the development of railroads and highways.

http://www.masshist.org/education/digital-classroom

The Massachusetts Historical Society Digital Classroom provides information on Massachusetts history with links to primary sources.

http://teacher.scholastic.com/researchtools/researchstarters/plymouth

Information on the Plymouth Colony, with many links to additional resources.

http://www.thefreedomtrail.org

Description of the historic sites along Boston's Freedom Trail.

http://www.mass.gov/portal/global-a-z-list.html

An official website for the government of Massachusetts, with information about various state agencies.

 # Text-Dependent Questions

1. What are the main agricultural crops grown in Massachusetts?
2. How did the blockade of 1807 and the War of 1812 affect the state of Massachusetts?
3. What were some of the social causes Bay Staters worked for during the mid-1800s?

 # Research Project

Find out more about the textile factories in Lowell in the mid-1800s. Write a short essay explaining what your life would be like if you were working in the mills at that time.

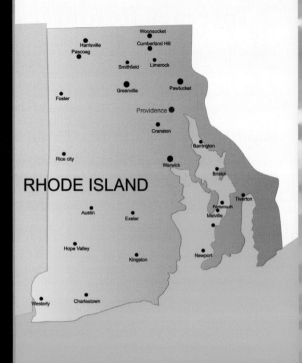

MASSACHUSETTS

Woonsocket
Harrisville
Pascoag
Cumberland Hill
Smithfield
Limerock
Greenville
Pawtucket
Foster
Providence
Cranston
Barrington
Rice city
Warwick
Bristol
RHODE ISLAND
Portsmouth
Melville
Tiverton
Austin
Exeter
Hope Valley
Kingston
Newport
Westerly
Charlestown

Rhode Island at a Glance

Area: 1,214 sq miles (3,144 sq km)[1]
The smallest state
Land: 1,034 sq mi (2,678 sq km)
Water: 180 sq mi (466 sq km)
Highest elevation: Jerimoth Hill,
812 feet (248 m)
Lowest elevation: Atlantic Ocean,
sea level (0 feet).

Statehood: May 29, 1790 (13th state)
Capital: Providence

Population: 1,055,173
(43rd largest state)[2]

State nickname: the Ocean State
State bird: Rhode Island Red
(chicken)
State flower: violet

[1] *U.S. Census Bureau*
[2] *U.S. Census Bureau, 2014 estimate*

Rhode Island

During the 16th century, Rhode Island was settled by European immigrants dissatisfied with life in the Puritan colonies of Massachusetts and Connecticut. They had no permission from the British to settle the land. The king had not appointed a governor to run the colony. The colonists were independent thinkers who developed their own laws. This independence was a disadvantage because it discouraged their settlements from coming together to form a regional government. But it was also a strength, because it encouraged the ideas that all people are created equal, should be able to freely express their beliefs, and should select their own leaders. This made colonial Rhode Island different from the rest of New England.

Geography

Rhode Island, sometimes nicknamed Little Rhody, is the smallest state in the nation. It forms a rough rectangle 48 miles (77 km) long and 37 miles (60 km) wide, and covers only 1,214 square miles (3,144 sq km). The state is bordered on the north and east by Massachusetts. Connecticut forms the border to the west. On the south, the Atlantic Ocean gives Rhode Island 40 miles (64

The Goat Island Lighthouse on Narragansett Bay. In the background is the Claiborne Pell Bridge, which connects Newport with the town of Jamestown on nearby Conanicut Island.

km) of coastline, although with all its bays and inlets, the state has almost 400 miles (640 km) of shoreline. Almost all Rhode Islanders live within a 30-minute drive of the Atlantic Ocean or Narragansett Bay, which is one reason why the state's official nickname is the Ocean State.

Rhode Island is made up of two geographic regions. The Coastal Lowland covers the easternmost third of the state and includes several off-shore islands (including Aquidneck, Conanicut, Block, Dutch, Hog, and a number of smaller islands). The coast-line is characterized by sandy beaches and salt marshes. Farther inland are low forest-covered hills.

The most prominent feature of the Coastal Lowland is Narragansett Bay, which extends from the Atlantic Ocean 28 miles (45 km) inland.

 # Words to Understand in This Chapter

Quaker—a Christian sect also known as the Religious Society of Friends. Quakers reject all church rituals, sacraments, and formal ministry. Their worship is mainly silent, although anyone in the congregation may speak if moved to do so by God.

smallpox—a contagious viral disease. Because Native Americans did not have a natural resistance to this disease, unlike Europeans, many died from smallpox.

Providence, the capital, is at the head of Narragansett Bay. Most of Rhode Island's important rivers, including the Blackstone, Pawtuxet, Potowomut, Woonasquatucket, and Providence rivers, drain into the bay.

The New England Upland covers the western two-thirds of the state. The forested hills are slightly higher here, although Jerimoth Hill, the highest point in the state, is only 812 feet (248 m) above sea level. The soil in the New England Upland region is poor and rocky, one reason why even in colonial times agriculture was never a major part of Rhode Island's economy.

The climate in Rhode Island is humid and generally milder than the rest of New England. The average January high temperature in Providence is 37°F (3°C), while the average high temperature in July is 83°F (28°C). Providence receives about 44 inches (112 cm) of rain each year, as well as roughly 33 inches (84 cm) of snow. The coastal areas and islands get less snow,

Snow-covered homes on a hillside in Providence.

while the northwest corner of the state receives slightly more.

History

When Europeans arrived in North America during the 16th century, Native Americans had been inhabiting what is now Rhode Island for thousands of years. The most powerful tribe in this region was the Narragansett. They dominated the Wampanoag and Niantic tribes that also lived in this region.

As in other parts of New England, the coming of Europeans was a disaster for Native Americans. Explorers carried diseases such as *smallpox* and measles that wiped out about 70 percent of the native populations, even before Europeans established permanent settlements in the region.

Rhode Island was settled by people who were unhappy living the Puritan communities in Massachusetts and Connecticut. When the Puritans came to the New World, they established a theocratic government. Church leaders were also the political leaders and judges. The laws of the colony were God's laws, as interpreted by Puritan leaders.

Roger Williams was a Puritan minister who believed that the church and the government should be separate. He also believed that men (but not women) should have a voice in choosing their leaders and in making laws. These ideas offended mainstream Puritans, who expelled Williams from the Massachusetts Bay Colony. In 1635, Williams and a small group of his followers founded Providence, the first permanent European settlement in what today is Rhode Island.

A statue of Roger Williams looks out over modern-day Providence from Prospect Terrace Park.

Williams was also different from most men of his time in the way he viewed Native Americans. He respected them, even though he did not approve of their religious beliefs. He spent several years living with a tribe in Massachusetts, learning its language and customs. Later he wrote a book called *A Key into the Language of America*, which described the language of the Narragansett people. When Williams founded the Providence Plantation colony, he purchased the land from the Native Americans, and insisted that future settlers do the same.

From the beginning, church and state were separate in Providence Plantation. People of all religious faiths could settle there. Laws were established by consent of the governed based on majority vote by the men in the colony. This was a shocking idea to people in the neighboring colonies, and attracted many who disagreed with the strict Puritans or were seeking religious freedom.

One of these dissenters was Anne Hutchinson, who was banished from Massachusetts for preaching that individuals could interpret the Bible for themselves. She and her family and friends moved to Aquidneck Island (at the time, it was called Rhode Island), where Roger Williams arranged for her to buy the land from the natives. In 1638 they established a settlement on the island called Portsmouth.

The next year, a disgruntled Hutchinson follower named William Coddington joined with a Baptist minister named John Clarke to establish another settlement on Aquidneck Island called Newport. Other religious dissenters soon arrived in the region, including **Quakers** and Jews.

 Did You Know?

In 1657, when the nearby Dutch colony of New Amsterdam refused to allow a ship full of Quakers to land, one Dutch minister wrote, "We suppose they went to Rhode Island, for that is the receptacle of all sorts of riff-raff people. . . . All the cranks of New England retire thither. . . . They are not tolerated in any other place."

The Jewish community in Newport built the first synagogue in North America, Touro Synagogue.

During the late 1630s and early 1640s, Massachusetts still claimed ownership of land where the Providence, Portsmouth, and Newport settlements were located. The issue was complicated by the fact that this territory had been settled without permission from the English government. This was during a time of civil war in England between supporters of the king and supporters of Parliament. To settle the dispute, Roger Williams and John Clarke sailed to England. In 1644, they received a land grant and charter from Parliament to create the Colony of Rhode Island and Providence Plantations. This united the various settlements in the region, and allowed them to choose their own government. In 1663, after the English king was restored to power, he granted the colony a royal charter that gave them the same rights.

Although Rhode Island was liberal in its attitude toward religious faith, it was deeply involved in the transatlantic slave trade. During the 17th and 18th centuries, many prominent Rhode Island families—including the Browns, for whom Brown University in Providence is named—made fortunes from slave trading. Newport in

The oldest Baptist Church in North America is located on College Hill in Providence.

particular was known as a port of entry for slaves captured in Africa. Most of these slaves were sent to plantations in the South, but some remained in Rhode Island to work on farms in the colony.

Eventually, the Rhode Island government passed a law that freed any slave who was born after March 1, 1784, when that slave reached the age of 21. Slaves born before this date were out of luck, however, and had to remain in slavery. The last slave in Rhode Island died in 1859.

Rhode Islanders were very involved in the rebellious colonial activities of the 1760s and 1770s leading up to the War for Independence. In 1772, Rhode Islanders attacked and burned the British warship HMS *Gaspee*, which had been stopping merchant ships in Narragansett Bay to look for smuggled goods on which British taxes had not been paid.

On May 4, 1776, the general assembly of Rhode Island voted to end its allegiance to the king of England. This day is celebrated as Rhode Island Independence Day. It came two months before the rest of the 13 American colonies declared their independence.

The British occupied Newport for three years during the Revolutionary War. They shut down all shipping from the port, which caused food shortages and hardship among residents of the colony. The only major battle fought in Rhode Island was an unsuccessful attempt to drive the British out of Newport in 1778. The British stayed for another year until their troops were needed elsewhere.

One Rhode Islander played a huge role in the success of the Continental Army. General Nathanael Greene from Warwick was one of George Washington's most trusted subordinates. During the early years of the war, Greene led troops in battles throughout New Jersey and Pennsylvania. In 1780, when the British destroyed an American army in the South and threatened to take control of the Southern colonies, Greene was

Nathanael Greene

sent to take command. He reorganized the Continental Army, and within a few months had turned the situation around. Troops under his command won major victories at Cowpens and Guilford Courthouse in 1781. This forced the British Army to retreat to Yorktown, Virginia, where it eventually surrendered.

Samuel Slater's original textile mill in Pawtucket was powered by falling water. Slater and his partners would eventually open successful mills elsewhere in Rhode Island, as well as in Massachusetts, Connecticut, and New Hampshire.

With the war over, Rhode Island continued its independent ways. The war had been financed by borrowing money from wealthy individuals. Now it was time to raise taxes to pay those debts. In 1787, Rhode Island representatives objected to some provisions in the proposed U.S. Constitution that would allow the federal government to levy taxes. They also wanted the Constitution to guarantee individual rights that they cherished, such as freedom of religion.

On May 29, 1790, Rhode Island became the last of the 13 original colonies to ratify the U.S. Constitution, by a vote of 34 to 32. The next year, 10 amendments—known as the Bill of Rights—were added to the Constitution to protect individual freedoms.

In the following years, Rhode Island prospered economically. Samuel Slater, called the "Father of the American Industrial Revolution," built the first water-powered textile mill on the Blackstone River in Pawtucket in 1790. Soon other mills were built along Rhode Island's many rivers.

The mills required labor, and immigrants provided the work force. Irish and French-Canadians came first, followed by immigrants from Italy and Portugal. From 1790 to 1860, the population of the state grew by 253 percent.

Rhode Island's dependency on cotton for its textile mills made its residents sympathetic to the South as the Civil War approached. State leaders resisted the idea of going to war and tried unsuccessfully to find a political solution to the issues that divided North and South. But 61 percent of Rhode Islanders voted for Abraham Lincoln in the 1860 presidential election, and the state was loyal to the Union when the Civil War began the following April. Rhode Island sent more than 25,000 men to fight during the war, and its factories manufactured supplies for the Union Army.

After the Civil War ended, the United States entered a period that has become known as the Gilded Age. Railroads expanded, factories boomed, immigrants poured into the country, and industrialists and financiers such

Did You Know?

The official name of Rhode Island is the State of Rhode Island and Providence Plantations. It is the smallest state and has the longest name of any state in the nation.

as Cornelius Vanderbilt, John D. Rockefeller, Andrew Carnegie, and J.P. Morgan made huge fortunes. Newport became a summer playground for wealthy families. The "cottages" they

Cornelius Vanderbilt's "summer cottage" in Newport, The Breakers, had 70 rooms. Today the mansion is a National Historic Landmark and is popular with tourists.

Governor John Chafee opens a section of I-95 in downtown Providence, 1964. Rerouting of highways led to urban renewal in many cities.

built were extravagant mansions. Some of these homes are open for public tours today.

Like the rest of the country, Rhode Island sent men to fight in World War I (1914–1918). After the war ended, many mills closed, the state experienced worker strikes, and unemployment increased even before the Great Depression sent unemployment skyrocketing. Although the state recov-

ered somewhat during World War II (1941–1945) by producing military supplies, it never regained its former status as a manufacturing center.

During the 1970s and early 1980s, Providence and other cities began to implement urban renewal projects. This revitalized the cities, and attracted new businesses to Rhode Island. Today, many of the state's residents commute to work in the Boston area.

Government

Rhode Island is governed from the State House in Providence. Elected officers of the executive branch include the governor, lieutenant governor, secretary of state, treasurer, and attorney general. Their term of office is four years. People elected to these positions can only serve two consecutive terms in the same position.

The legislature of Rhode Island, called the General Assembly, consists of two houses. The Senate has 38 members and the House of Representatives has 75 members. All members are elected for two-year terms in even-numbered years.

The judicial branch is made up of the Supreme Court, Superior Court, District Court, and lower courts such as Family Court and Workers' Compensation Court. The governor nominates a judge when a vacancy occurs on the Supreme Court. The judge must then be approved by the both houses of the General Assembly. Supreme Court Justices serve for life. Vacancies in lower courts are filled by nomination of the governor and approval by the Senate.

Rhode Island is divided into five counties, but differs from 48 other states in having no county governments. Local government is handled

Lincoln Chafee represented Rhode Island in the U.S. Senate from 1999 until 2007, and was elected governor of Rhode Island in 2011, serving one term. He is the son of former Connecticut governor and U.S. Senator John Chafee.

by eight cities and 31 municipalities.

The state sends two senators and two representatives to the U.S. Congress, giving the state four electoral votes. Considering the size of Rhode Island's population, the people of this state are well represented in the Electoral College. There is one Rhode Island elector for about every 265,000 people. By comparison, large states like California, Texas, and New York have about one elector for every 670,000 people.

The Economy

In colonial times, Newport dominated the economy of Rhode Island. Its excellent harbor encouraged fishing and trade. After America became

The Rhode Island State House in Providence was built in 1904.

Near downtown Providence, the Moshassuck and the Woonasquatucket Rivers come together to form the Providence River, which empties into the Narragansett Bay.

independent from Great Britain, Rhode Island developed into a manufacturing state. Instead of transporting slaves, ships in the Newport harbor carried cotton from the South to be spun and woven into cloth.

Today, the U. S. Navy is a large presence along the Rhode Island coast. Newport is the home of the Naval Undersea Warfare Center, which develops submarine technology for the 21st century. Other defense-related industries such as Raytheon specialize in manufacturing communication, detection, and underwater sound equipment. The state also produces aircraft components for military use.

Hasbro, one of the world's leading toy-making companies, was founded in Pawtucket in 1923. It is still headquartered there. Some of the toys and games the company produces include Monopoly, Transformers, Play-Doh, Mr. Potato Head, G.I. Joe, and Nerf.

Rhode Island's diverse universities are among the largest employers in the state. Brown University and the University of Rhode Island offer traditional undergraduate and graduate programs. Rhode Island School of Design is one of the country's most prestigious fine arts schools. Johnson & Wales University prepares students for the culinary and hospitality industries.

Tourism also contributes to the state's economy. The state has more than 100 beaches, as well as many historic sites. About 41,000 people in Rhode Island work in the tourism industry.

The median household income in Rhode Island is $56,102, slightly higher than the national average. Poverty is a problem in Rhode Island, however, as more than 13 percent of the state's residents have incomes below the poverty level.

The People

In the census of 1800, 69,122 people lived in Rhode Island. By 2014, that number had grown to more than 1 million residents. This makes Rhode Island the 43rd most populous state in the nation. However, Rhode Island is densely populated, with more people per square mile than every state except New Jersey.

In 2014, 85.6 percent of the population self-identified as white, but this included 13 percent who also identified as Hispanic or Latino. Blacks made up only 7.5 percent of the population, a much smaller percentage than the 13.2 percent of the overall U.S. population.

Rhode Islanders, like the other residents of southern New England, tend to be slightly more religious than the nation as a whole. Forty-five percent of the population are Roman Catholics, 9 percent belong to other Christian churches, and about 1 percent practice other religions. There has been a Jewish community in Rhode Island since the 1650s, and the first synagogue in America was built in Newport in 1753.

Major Cities

Rhode Island is so small that it has only eight cities. ***Providence***, with its gold-domed capital, is the largest city in the state and one of the oldest in the nation. At one time, Providence was a manufacturing center. Today, the emphasis is on service industries.

Some Famous Rhode Islanders

For a small state, Rhode Island has produced a lot of talented people. Gilbert Stuart (1775–1828) may not be a household name, but his work can be found all over America. Stuart was born in Saunderstown and moved to Newport as a child. Artistically gifted, he became one of the most respected painters of his time. He painted more than 1,000 portraits, including one of George Washington that appears on the $1 bill.

U.S. Navy Commodore Oliver Hazard Perry (1785–1819), born in South Kingstown, was a hero of the War of 1812. His small fleet defeated the British at the Battle of Lake Erie in September 1813, and he played an important leadership role in many other battles during the war.

George M. Cohan (1878–1942), a Providence native, wrote, acted in, and produced Broadway musicals and non-musical plays. He also composed more than 300 songs, including "You're a Grand Old Flag" and "Give my Regards to Broadway."

Oliver Hazard Perry

Meredith Vieira

More recently, Rhode Island has produced several well-known television personalities. Meredith Vieira, born in Providence in 1953, spent 11 years as the host of *Who Wants to be a Millionaire* and nine years on *The View*. In 2014, her own daytime talk show, *The Meredith Vieira Show*, began airing.

The View seems to like hosts from Rhode Island. Elisabeth Hasselbeck, born in Cranston in 1977, spent 10 years on the show before moving to *Fox and Friends*.

Another Cranston-born native, Olivia Culpo (b. 1992), was crowned Miss Rhode Island 2012 in the first pageant she ever entered. She went on to win the title of Miss USA 2012 and Miss Universe 2012. She was the first person from the United States to win the Miss Universe title in 15 years.

The city has eight hospitals and seven institutions of higher learning.

Warwick is the second-largest city in Rhode Island. It was founded in 1642 by Samuel Gorton after he was driven out of three other New England colonies (Plymouth, Portsmouth, and Providence) because of his outspoken contempt for ministers and the law. Today, Warwick is the site of the state's major airport, T. F. Green Airport, and boasts 39 miles of coastline for recreation.

Almost one-third of the people living in *Cranston*, the third-largest city, are of Italian-American descent. The city is home to several companies that make jewelry and watches. In 2010, the Pawtuxet River flooded, damaging much of downtown Cranston.

Newport is located on Aquidneck Island, the largest island in Narragansett Bay. It draws visitors from all over the world who come to tour the mansions built as summer homes by some of the wealthiest Americans during the late 1800s.

Further Reading

Aller, Susan Bivens. *Anne Hutchinson*. Minneapolis: Lerner Publications, 2010.

Burgan, Michael. *Rhode Island*. New York: Children's Press, 2014.

Greene, Meg. *The Everything Founding Fathers Book: All You Need to Know About the Men Who Shaped America*. Avon, Mass.: Adams Media, 2011.

Marsh, Carole. *Rhode Island History Projects: 30 Cool, Activities, Crafts, Experiments & More for Kids to Do*. Peachtree City, Ga.: Gallopade International, 2003.

Mierka, Greg. *Nathanael Greene: The General Who Saved the Revolution*. Stockton, N.J.: OTTN Publishing, 2007.

Internet Resources

http://sos.ri.gov/kidszone

Office of the Secretary of State official kids' website with interesting historical facts, tourism information, and games.

http://www.visitrhodeisland.com

Official website of the Rhode Island Tourism Division

http://www.info.ri.gov/browse.php?choice=show_az&letter=a

A complete list of all Rhode Island government agencies with links to their websites.

http://sos.ri.gov/archon

Digital gateway to the state's collection of documents

http://www.rihs.org

Website of the Rhode Island State Historical Society.

 # Text-Dependent Questions

1. Why was Rhode Island reluctant to ratify the United States Constitution?
2. What role did Samuel Slater play in the development of industry in Rhode Island?

 # Research Project

Rhode Island insisted that certain rights and freedoms be guaranteed in the U.S. Constitution. To satisfy this demand, the Constitutional Convention agreed to add ten amendments to the U.S. Constitution. These amendments are known as the Bill of Rights. Research the Bill of Rights and explain what these freedoms are.

Index

Numbers in **bold italics** refer to captions.

Series Glossary of Key Terms

bicameral—having two legislative chambers (for example, a senate and a house of representatives).

cede—to yield or give up land, usually through a treaty or other formal agreement.

census—an official population count.

constitution—a written document that embodies the rules of a government.

delegation—a group of persons chosen to represent others.

elevation—height above sea level.

legislature—a lawmaking body.

precipitation—rain and snow.

term limit—a legal restriction on how many consecutive terms an office holder may serve.